ALFRED'S BASIC ADULT
ALL-TIME FAVORITES

WILLARD A. PALMER • MORTON MANUS • DENNIS ALEXANDER

ALL-TIME FAVORITES is designed to supplement ALFRED'S BASIC ADULT PIANO COURSE, Level 1. This volume may also be used as supplementary enrichment with any piano course, and for those who know how to play and just want to enjoy wonderful music.

A glance at the contents of this book will show the great variety of pieces offered here. Included are Sing-Along Favorites, Folk and Country Songs, arrangements of well-known Classics, plus Holiday, Seasonal, and Songs for Special Occasions. The timeless appeal of these familiar pieces will provide hours of enjoyment for the pianist and listener, and will reinforce and broaden the musical skills of every piano student. They are placed roughly in order of difficulty.

ACH, DU LIEBER AUGUSTINE

German Folk Song

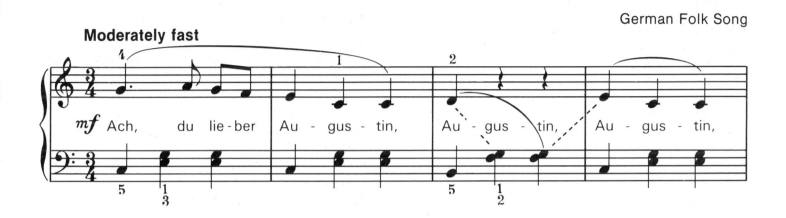

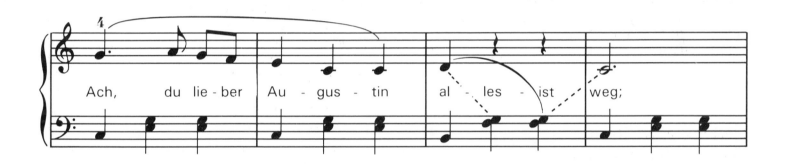

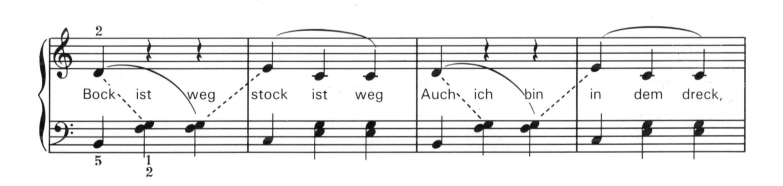

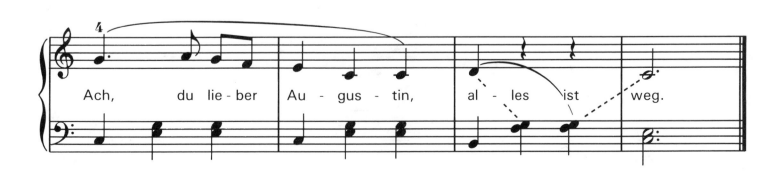

FINLANDIA
(Theme)

Use after page 57.

Jan Sibelius

Moderately slow

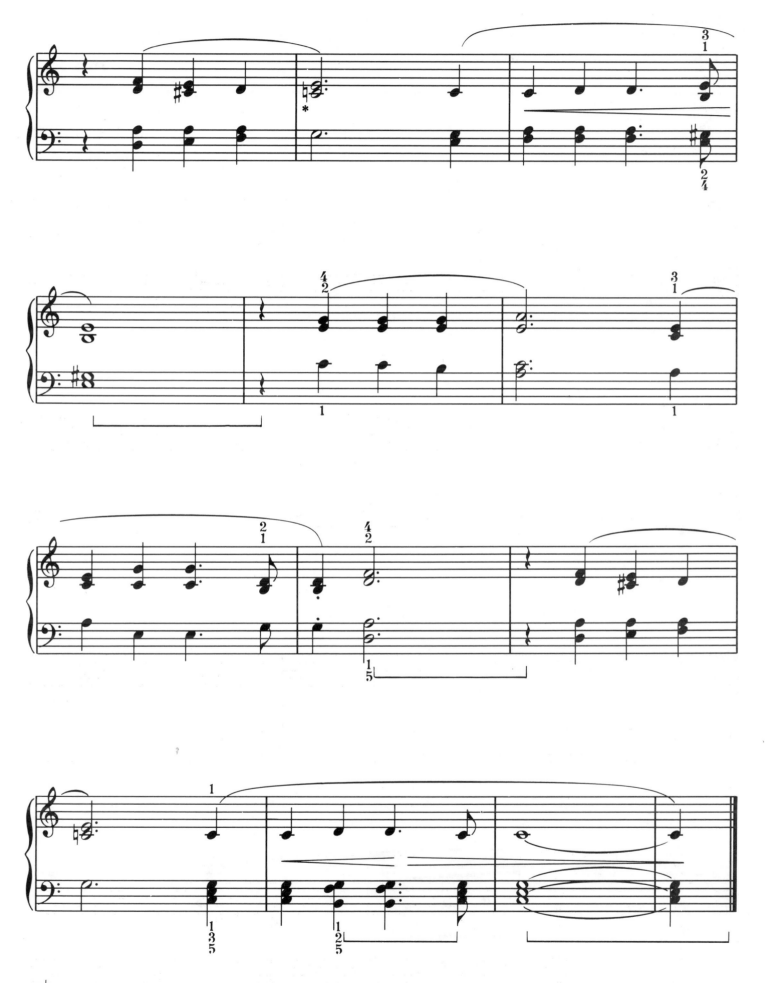

*♮ This is a natural sign. A note after a natural sign is always a white key. It is used here to remind you to play C instead of C♯.

6

SONATA PATHETIQUE
(Theme from the 2nd Movement)

Use after page 58.

Ludwig van Beethoven

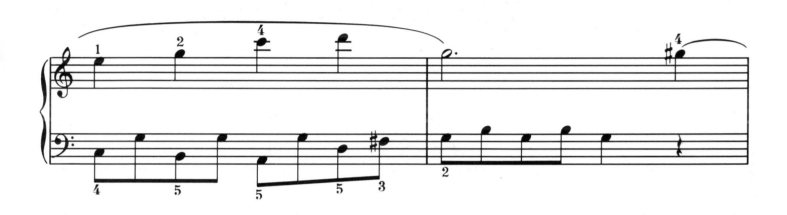

FRANKIE AND JOHNNY

Use after page 60.

Moderately

Frank-ie and John - nie were lov - ers! Oh Lord - y, how they could

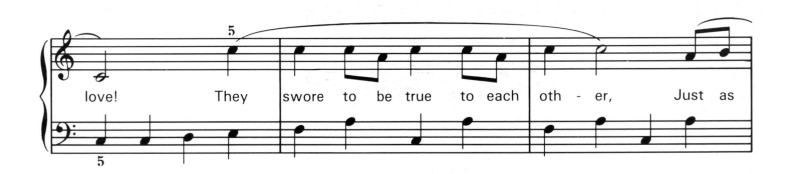

love! They swore to be true to each oth - er, Just as

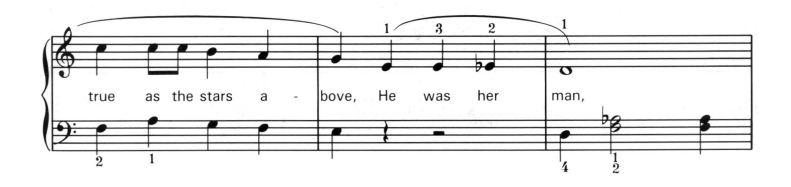

true as the stars a - bove, He was her man,

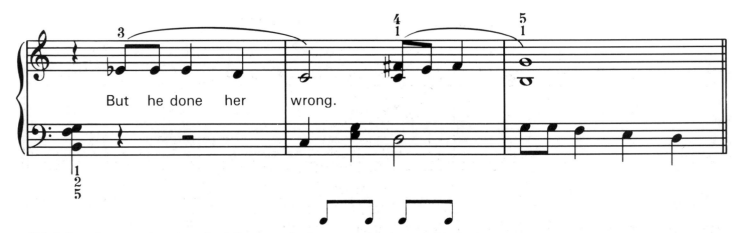

But he done her wrong.

*Eighth notes may be played a bit unevenly, long   short, long   short.

Frank-ie went down to the cor - ner, Or-dered a buck - et of

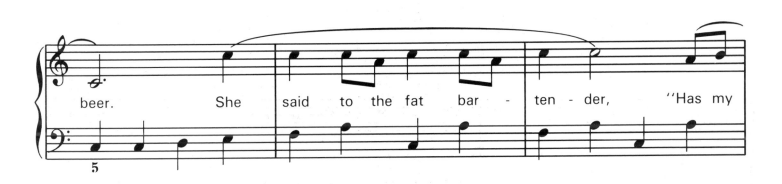

beer. She said to the fat bar - ten - der, "Has my

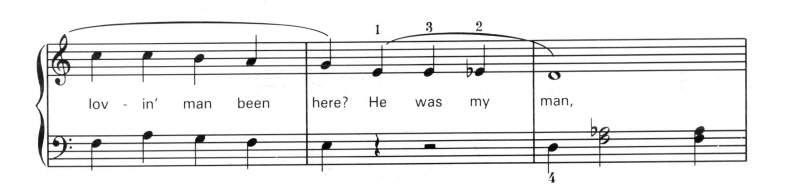

lov - in' man been here? He was my man,

ritardando

But he's done me wrong!" (tremolo)*

Tremolo: Alternate the two notes in each hand as rapidly as possible.

LULLABY

Use after page 58.

Johannes Brahms

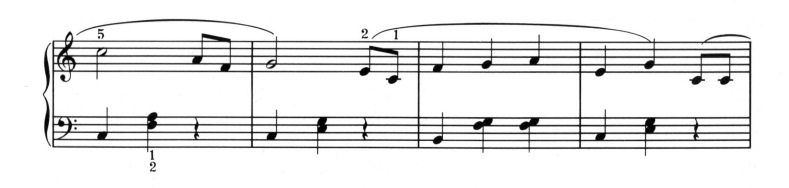

PIANO CONCERTO No. 2
(Theme from the 3rd Movement)

Sergei Rachmaninoff

*♮ natural sign means play white key B instead of B♭.

Use after page 62.

HUNGARIAN RHAPSODY NO. 2
(Theme)

Franz Liszt

Not too fast, with rhythmic emphasis

A little faster

♮ natural sign means play white key F instead of F♯.
> accent sign. Play with special emphasis.

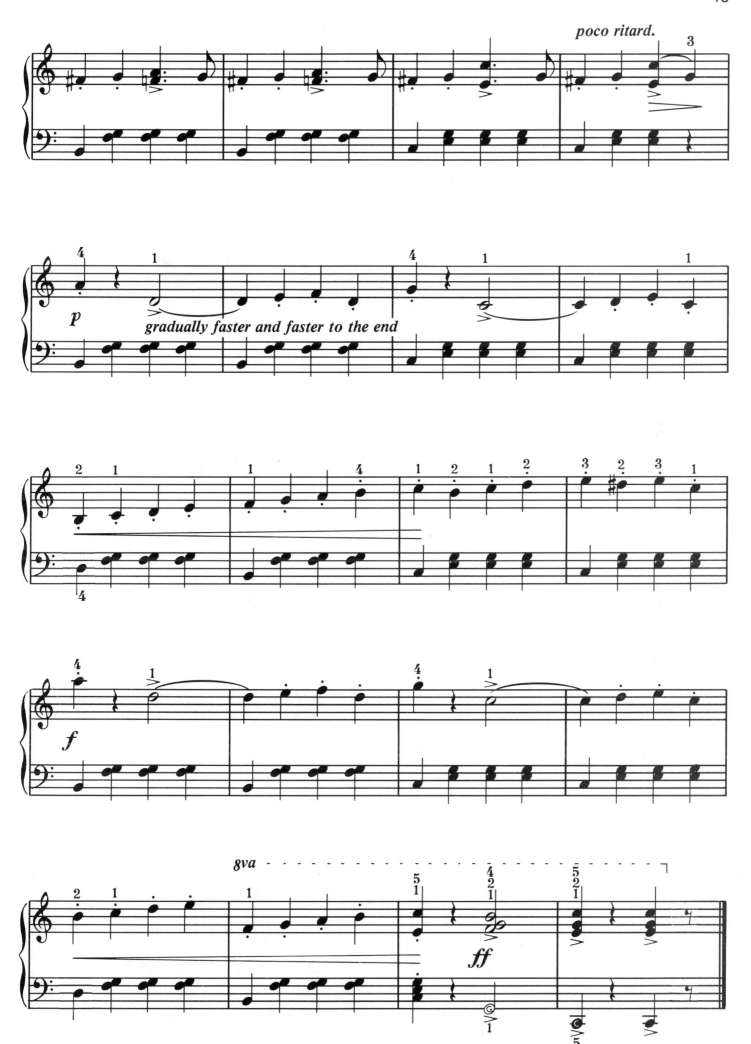

MY GAL SAL

Use after page 62.

Paul Dresser

Moderately

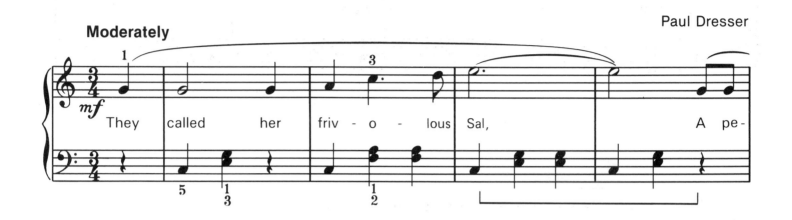

They called her friv - o - lous Sal, A pe-

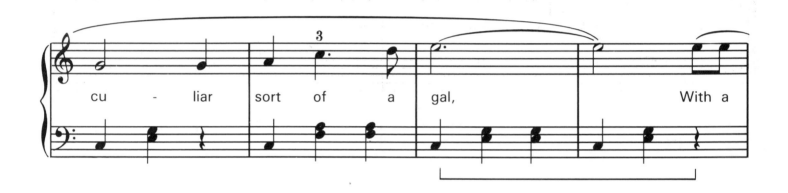

cu - liar sort of a gal, With a

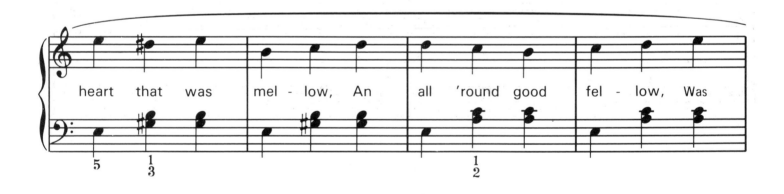

heart that was mel - low, An all 'round good fel - low, Was

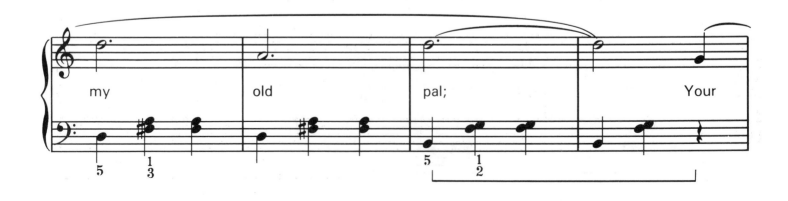

my old pal; Your

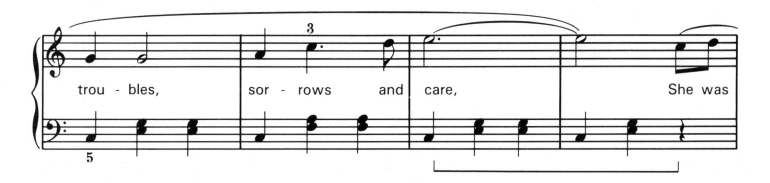

trou - bles, sor - rows and care, She was

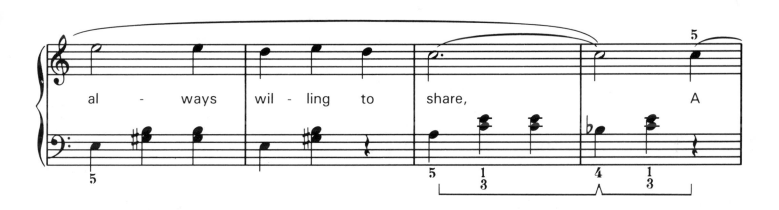

al - ways wil - ling to share, A

wild sort of dev - il, But dead on the lev - el, was

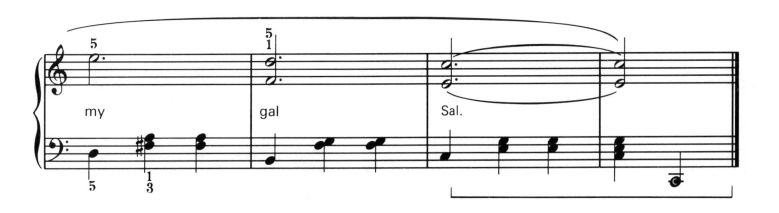

my gal Sal.

MY WILD IRISH ROSE

Use after page 63.

Chauncy Olcott

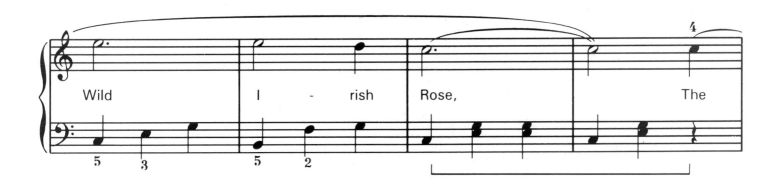

Wild   I - rish   Rose,   The

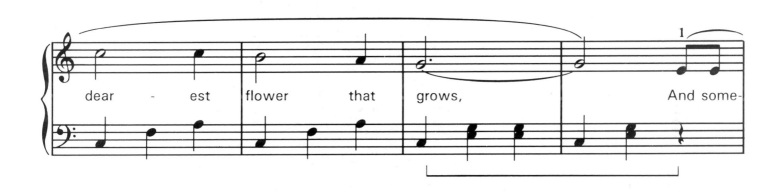

dear - est   flower   that   grows,   And some-

day   for   my   sake,   She   may   let   me   take   the

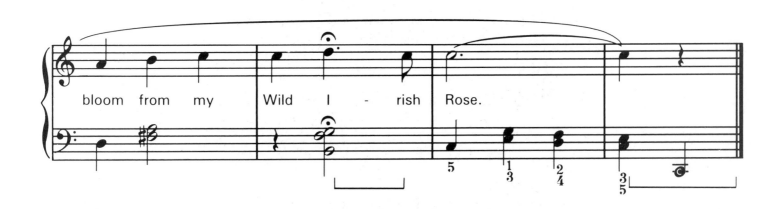

bloom   from   my   Wild   I - rish   Rose.

TAKE ME OUT TO THE BALLGAME

Use after page 68.

Words by Jack Norworth
Music by Albert von Tilzer

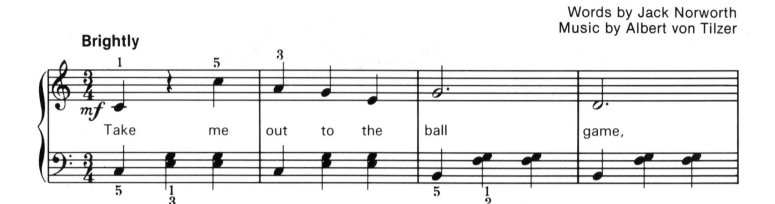

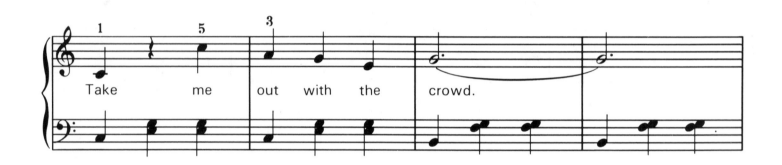

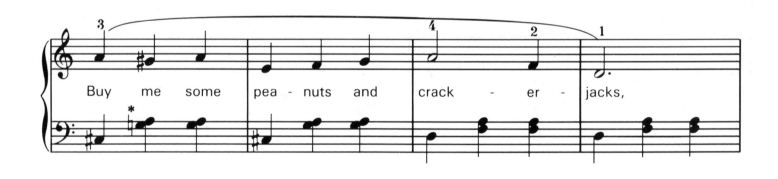

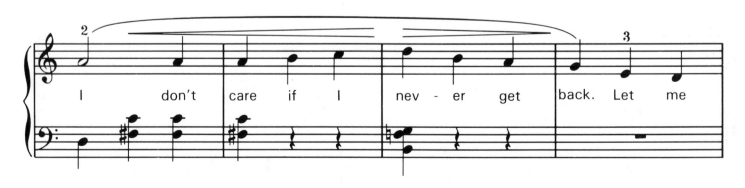

*♮ natural sign. LH plays white key G while RH plays G♯.

root, root, root for the home team, If

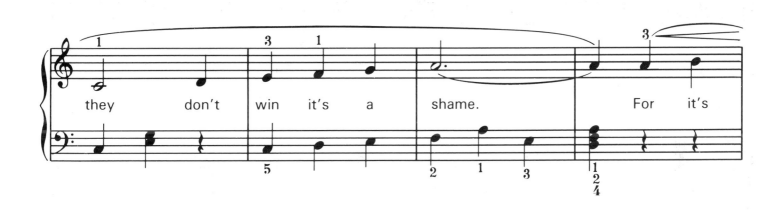

they don't win it's a shame. For it's

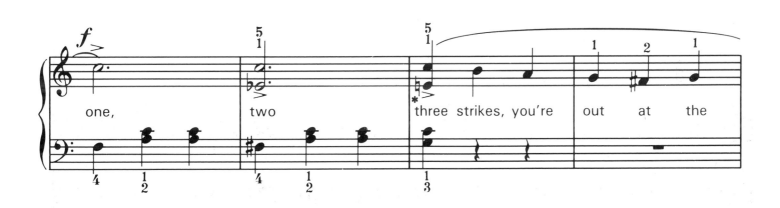

one, two three strikes, you're out at the

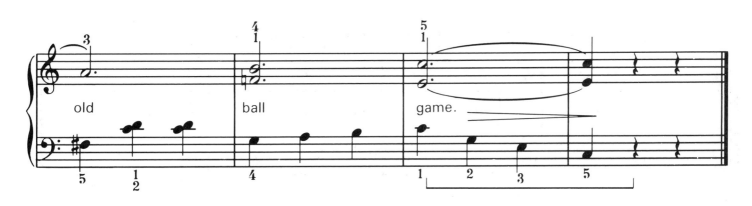

old ball game.

*Play white key E instead of E♭.

BRIDAL CHORUS
from "Lohengrin"

Use after page 68.

Richard Wagner

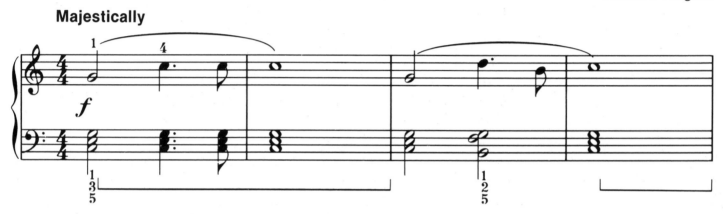

(to next strain)

Fine

D.C. al Fine*

*D.C. al Fine means repeat from the beginning, and play to the Fine (end).

IN THE GOOD OLD SUMMER TIME

Use after page 68.

Words by Ron Shields
Music by George Evans

Moderate waltz tempo

* ♮ natural sign. Play white key F instead of F♯.

hold   her   hand   and   she   holds   yours,   And

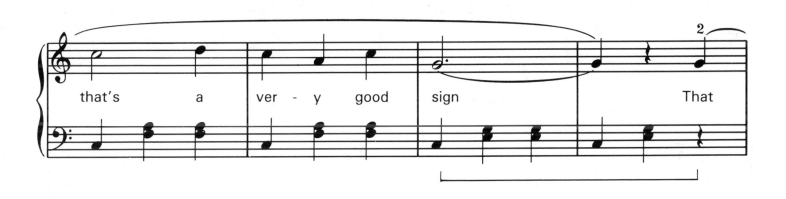

that's   a   ver - y   good   sign   That

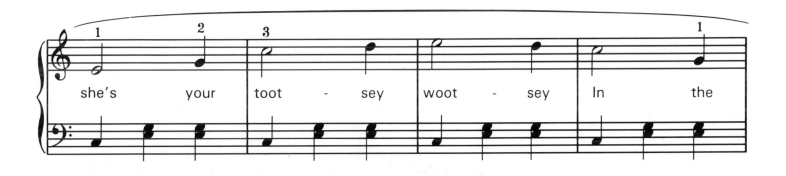

she's   your   toot - sey   woot - sey   In   the

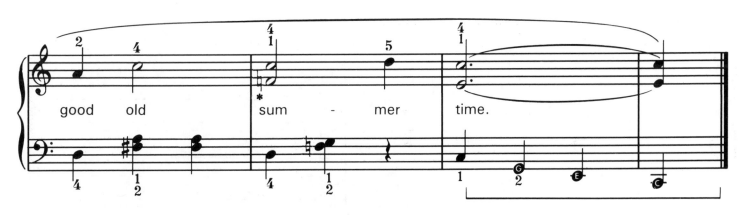

good   old   sum - mer   time.

*The natural sign reminds you to play white key F instead of F♯.

ROMANCE FROM THE SERENADE
"Eine Kleine Nachtmusik"
(A Little Night Music)

Use after page 68.

Wolfgang Amadeus Mozart

Moderately slow

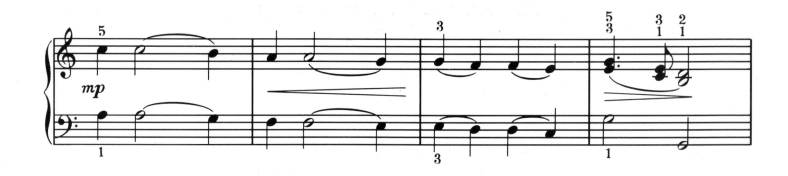

* ♮ natural sign. The natural sign cancels the F♯.

CINDY

Use after page 72.

Traditional

Moderately fast square dance tempo

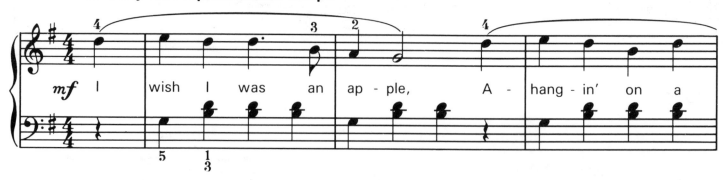

mf I wish I was an ap - ple, A - hang - in' on a

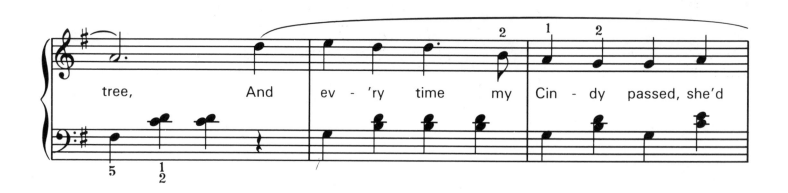

tree, And ev - 'ry time my Cin - dy passed, she'd

take a bite of me. She told me that she

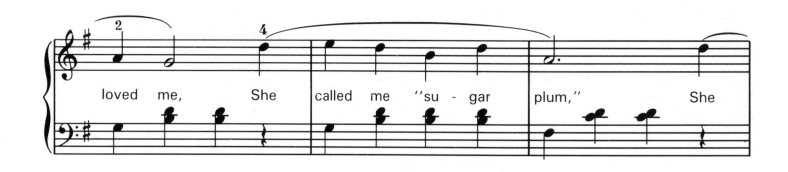

loved me, She called me "su - gar plum," She

threw her arms a-round me, I thought my time had come.

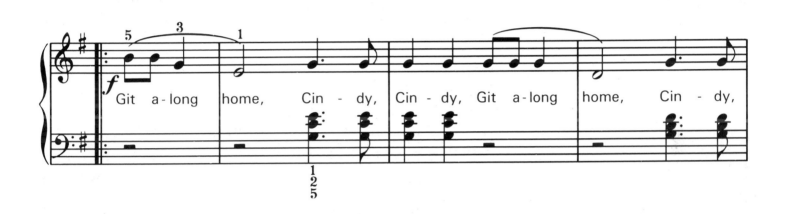

Git a-long home, Cin - dy, Cin - dy, Git a-long home, Cin - dy,

Cin - dy, Git a-long home, Cin - dy, Cin - dy, I'll

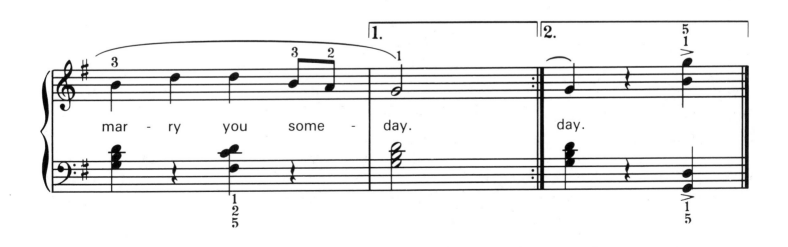

mar - ry you some - day. day.

Use after page 73.

Plaisir d'Amour
(The Joy of Love)

This piece was made into a popular song by Elvis Presley.

Giovanni Martini

Moderately slow

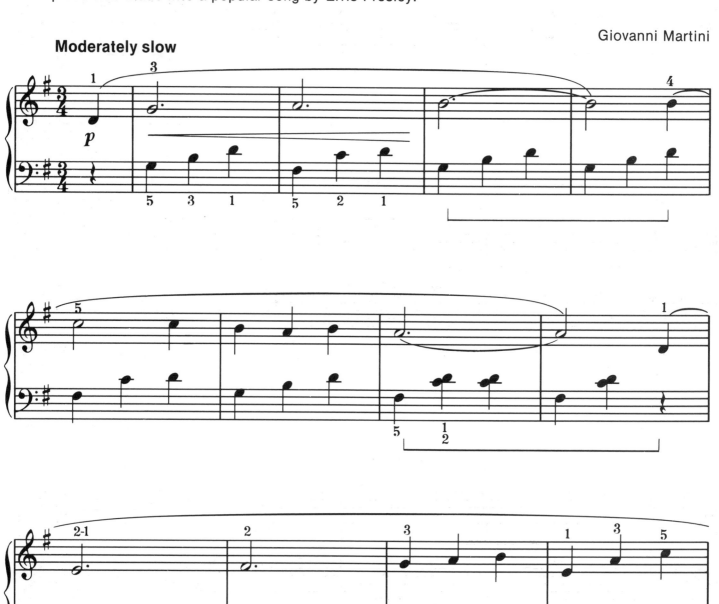

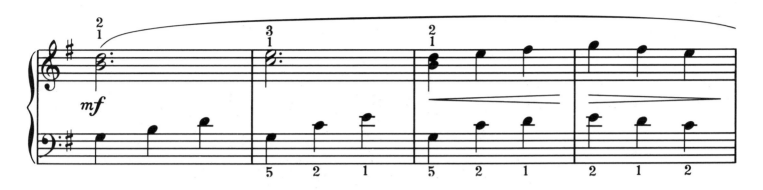

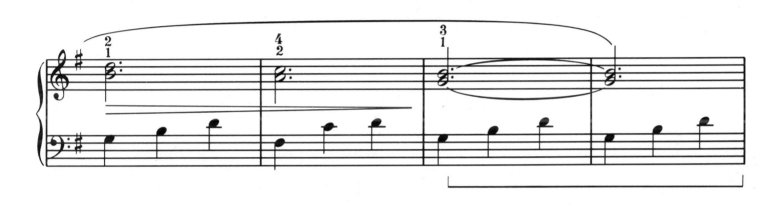

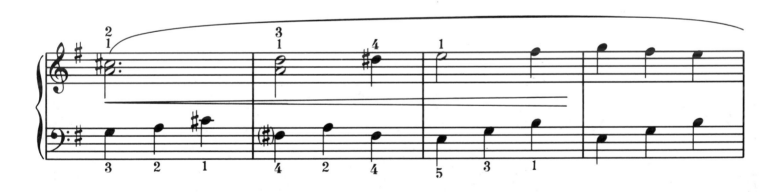

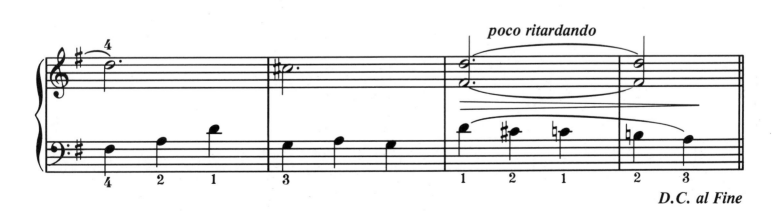

D.C. al Fine

LET ME CALL YOU SWEETHEART

Use after page 73.

Words by Beth Slater Whitson
Music by Leo Friedman

Moderate waltz tempo

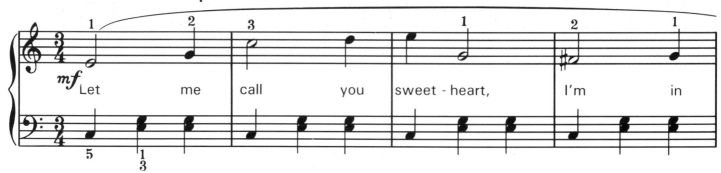

mf Let me call you sweet-heart, I'm in

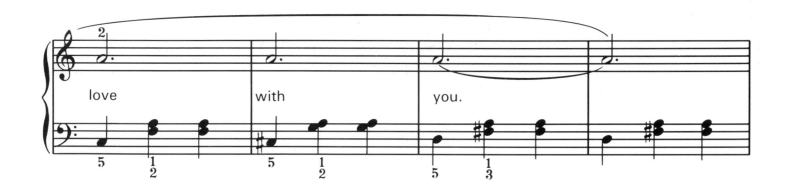

love with you.

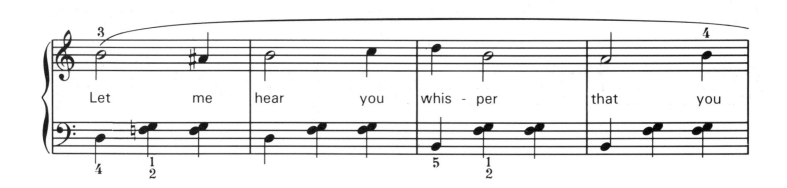

Let me hear you whis-per that you

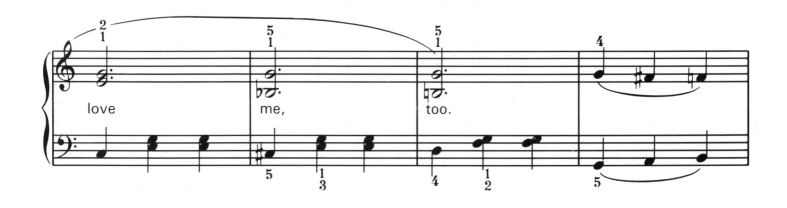

love me, too.

Keep the love - light glow - ing in your

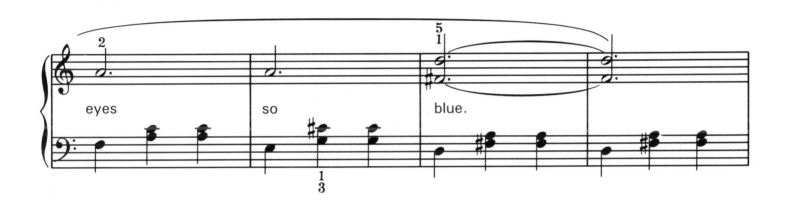

eyes so blue.

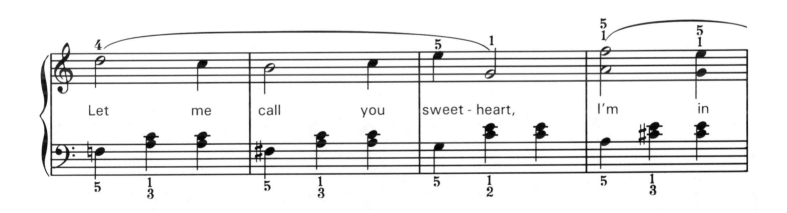

Let me call you sweet - heart, I'm in

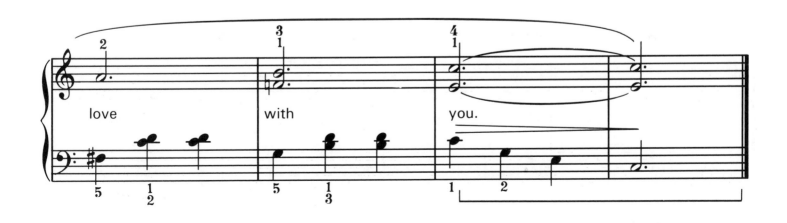

love with you.

WHEN IRISH EYES ARE SMILING

Use after page 73.

Words by Chauncy Olcott and George Graff, Jr.
Music by Ernest R. Ball

Moderately

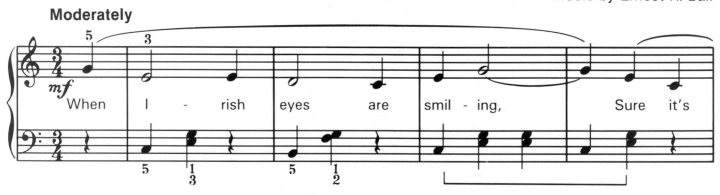

When I - rish eyes are smil - ing, Sure it's

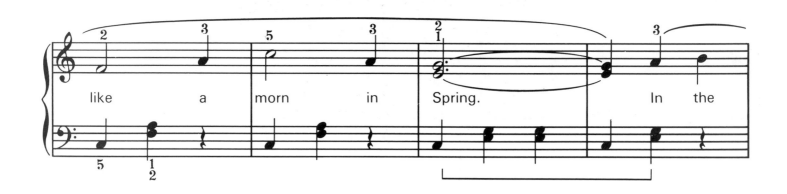

like a morn in Spring. In the

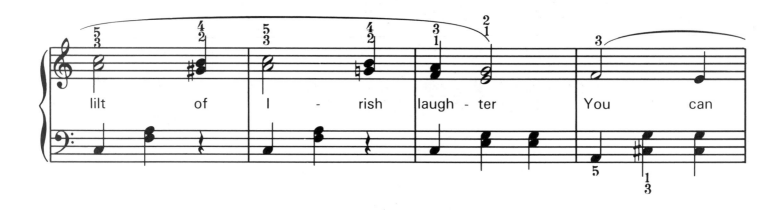

lilt of I - rish laugh - ter You can

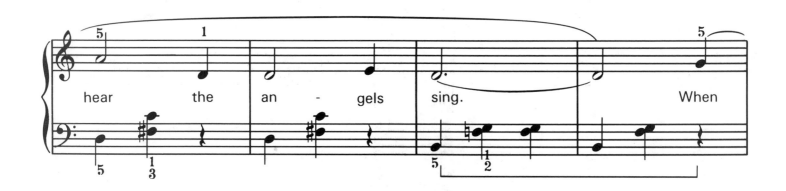

hear the an - gels sing. When

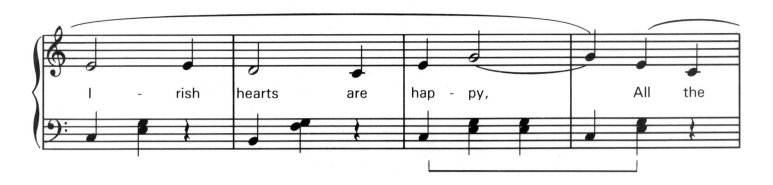

I - rish hearts are hap - py, All the

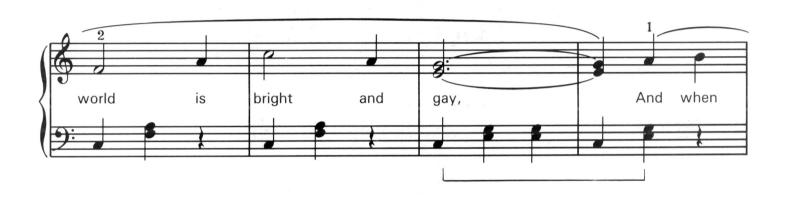

world is bright and gay, And when

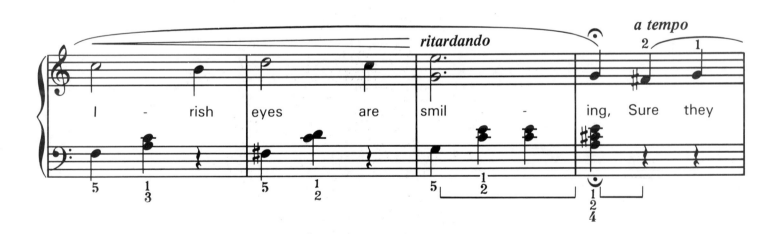

ritardando   *a tempo*

I - rish eyes are smil - ing, Sure they

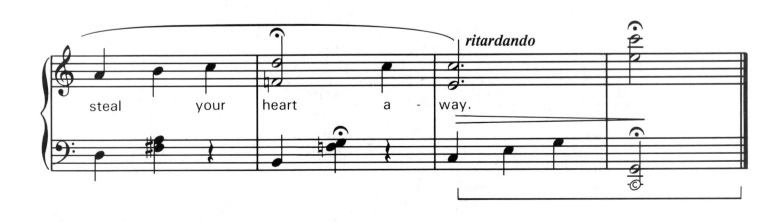

ritardando

steal your heart a - way.

Use after page 73.

CUDDLE UP A LITTLE CLOSER

Words by O. A. Hauerbach
Music by Karl Hoschna

*The eighth notes may be played a bit unevenly, long   short, long   short.

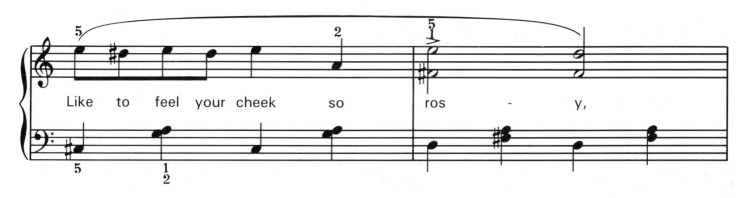

Like to feel your cheek so ros - y,

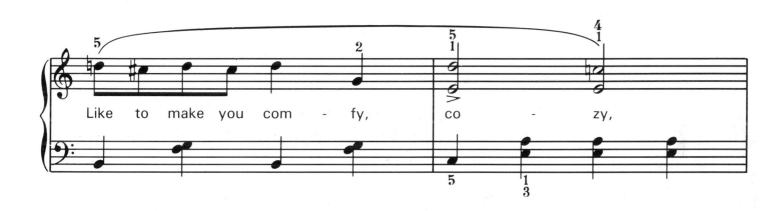

Like to make you com - fy, co - zy,

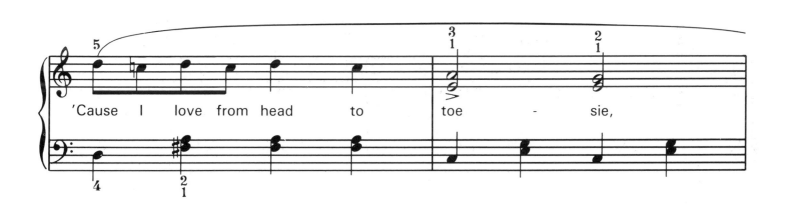

'Cause I love from head to toe - sie,

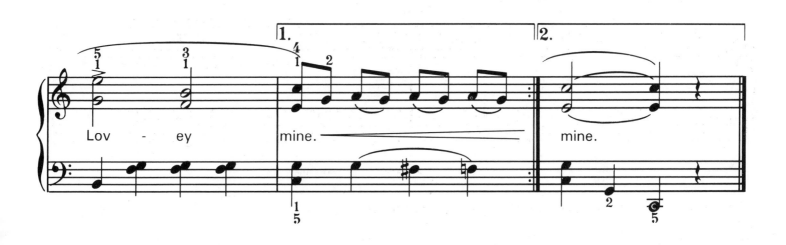

Lov - ey mine. mine.

MY MELANCHOLY BABY

Use after page 73.

Words by George A. Norton
Music by Ernie Burnett

Very slowly and freely

Come to me, my mel - an - chol - y ba - by,

Cud - dle up and don't be blue;

All your fears are fool - ish fan - cy, may - be,

You know, dear, that I'm in love with you.

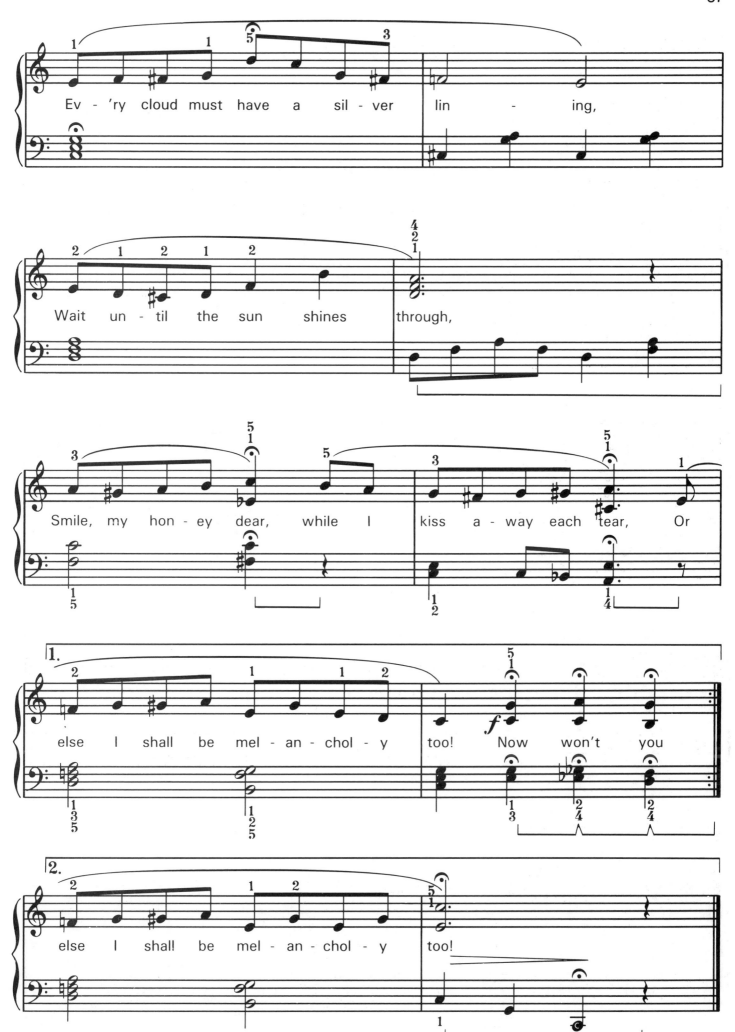

LIEBESTRAUM
(Theme from No. 3)

Use after page 73.

Franz Liszt

Moderately, with feeling

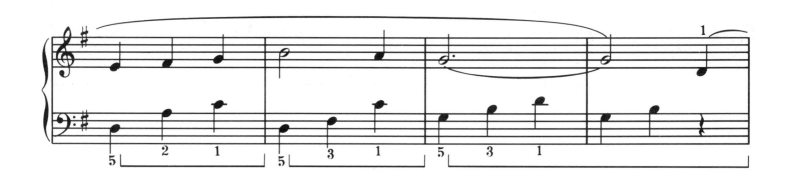

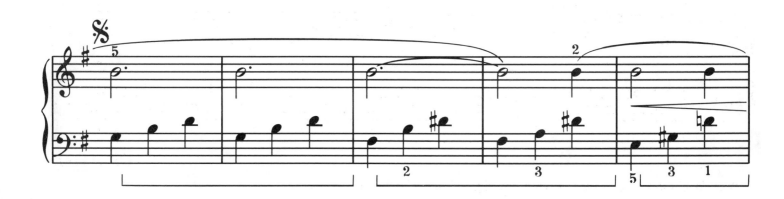

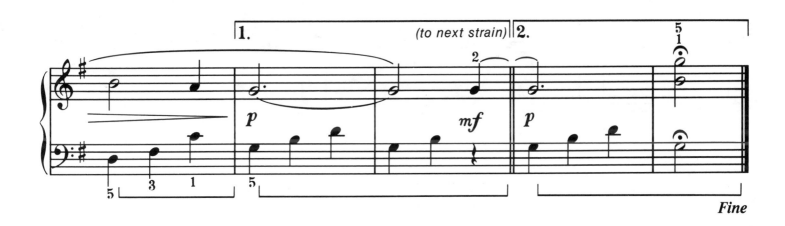

Fine

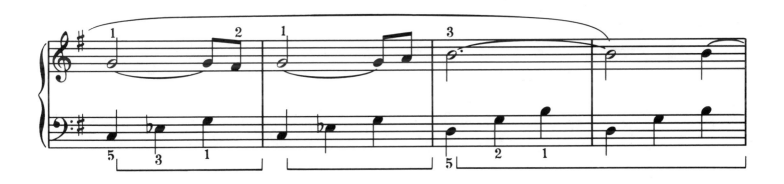

D.S. %% al Fine

*D.S. %% al Fine means repeat from the sign %% and play to the Fine (end).

BY THE LIGHT OF THE SILVERY MOON

Use after page 73.

With a rhythmic bounce (not too fast)

Words by Ed Madden
Music by Gus Edwards

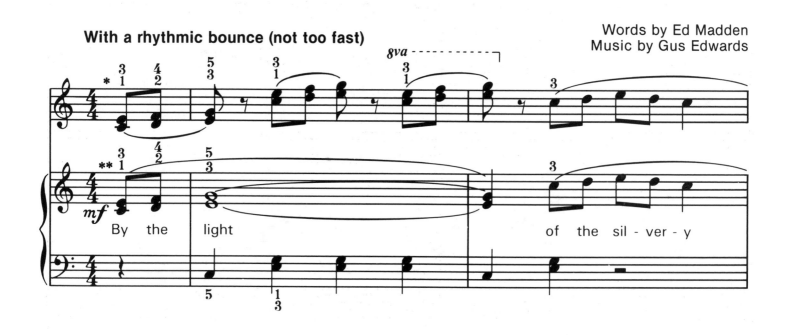

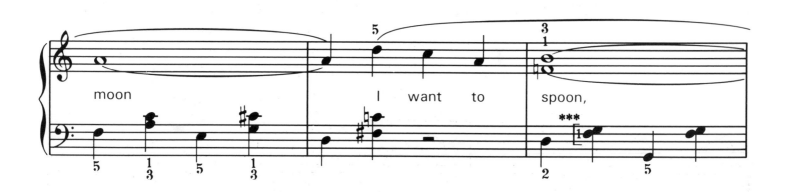

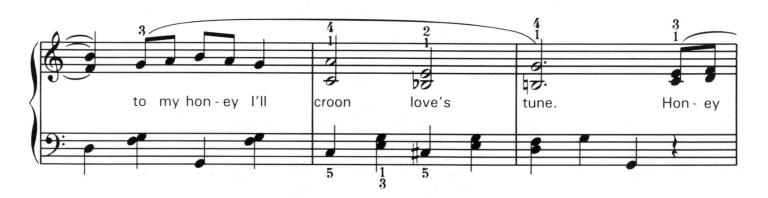

*OPTIONAL: Play notes on the upper treble staff instead of the regular staff.

**The eighth notes may be played a bit unevenly, long   short, long   short.
***Play the F & G with the side tip of the thumb.

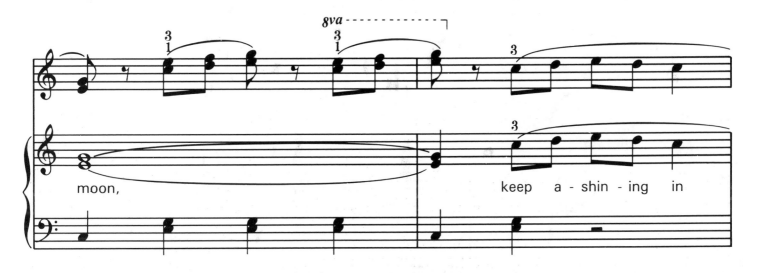

moon, keep a - shin - ing in

June. Your sil - v'ry beams will bring love

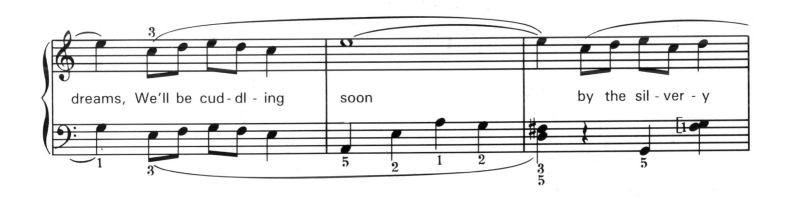

dreams, We'll be cud - dl - ing soon by the sil - ver - y

moon.

THE CAMPTOWN RACES

Use after page 68.

Stephen Foster

Moderately fast

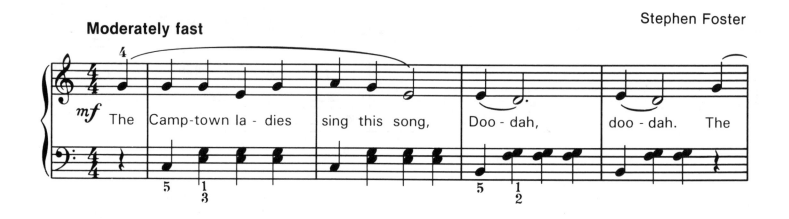

The Camp-town la - dies sing this song, Doo - dah, doo - dah. The

Camp-town race track's five miles long, Oh, doo - dah dey.

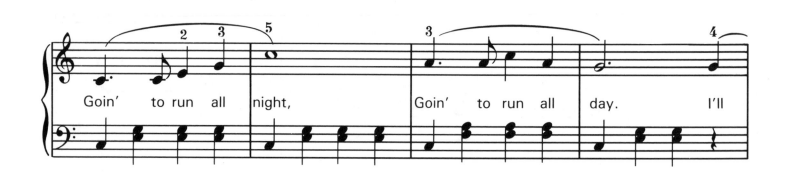

Goin' to run all night, Goin' to run all day. I'll

bet my mon-ey on the bob - tail nag, Some-bod-y bet on the bay.

Take Me Home, Country Roads

Use after page 73.

Words and Music by Bill Danoff,
Taffy Nivert and John Denver

Bright Country tempo

Lyrics under the staves:

I hear her voice, In the morn - in' hour she

calls me, The ra - di - o re - minds me of my

home far a - way, And driv - in' down the road I get a

feel - in' that I should have been home yes - ter - day, yes - ter

day. Coun - try

CODA *ritardando*

*D.S. 𝄋 al ⊕ Coda**

D.S. 𝄋 al ⊕ Coda means repeat from the sign 𝄋 and play to the sign ⊕, then skip to the CODA (ending).

Use after page 73.

LONDONDERRY AIR

Traditional

Moderately slow

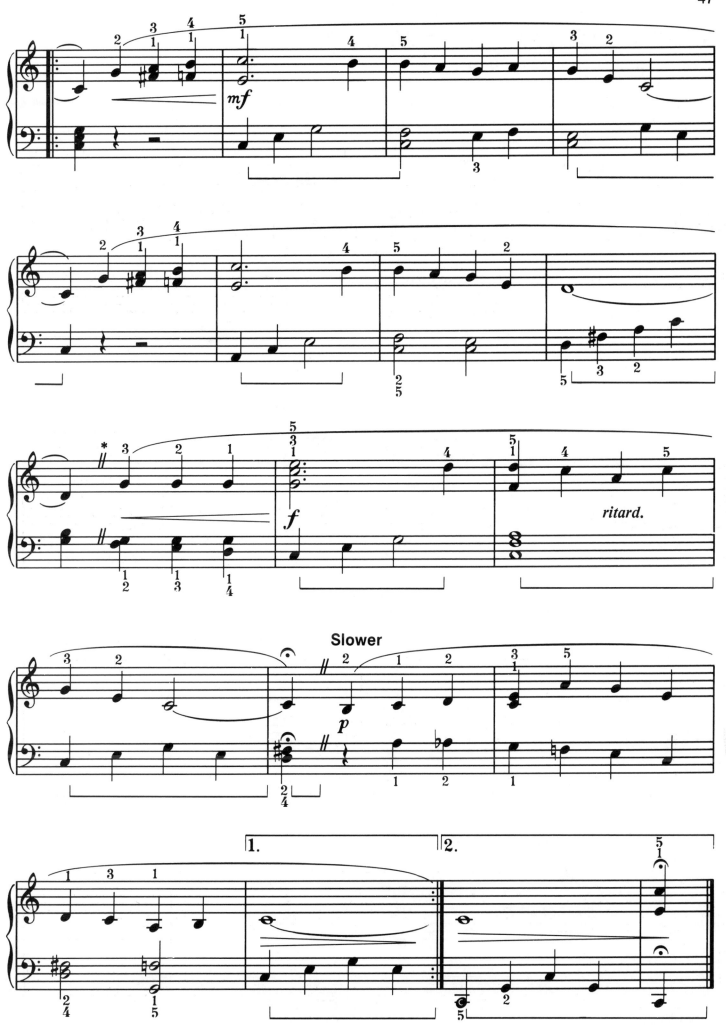

*‖ = Make a very slight pause.

MY HEART AT THY SWEET VOICE

(from "Sampson and Delilah)

Use after page 73.

Camille Saint-Saëns

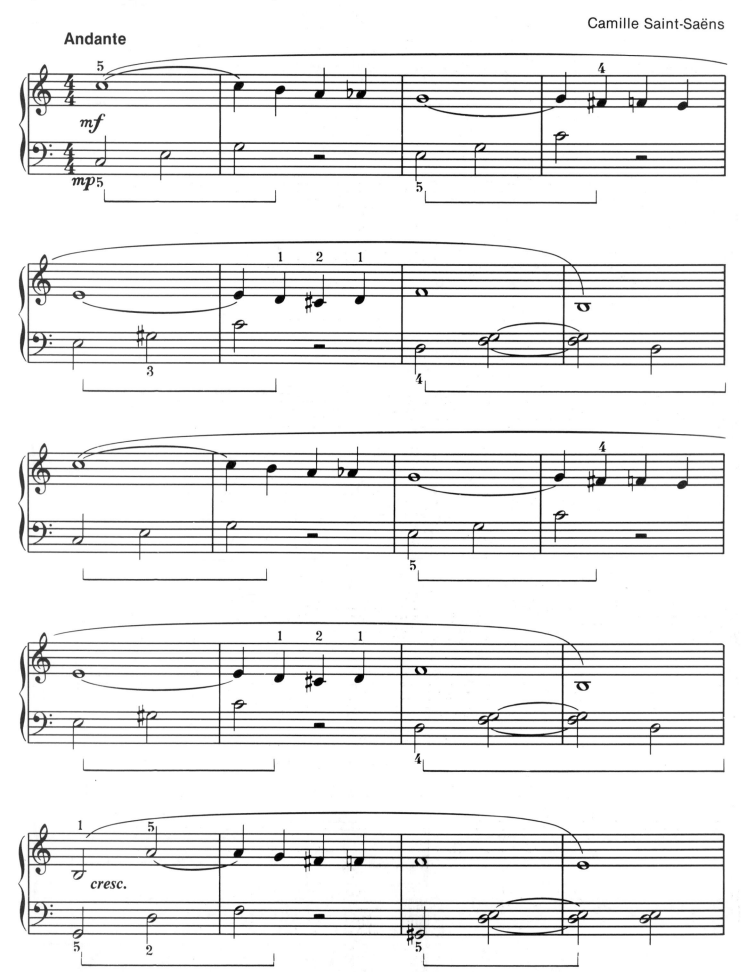

CLEMENTINE

Use after page 74.

Percy Montross

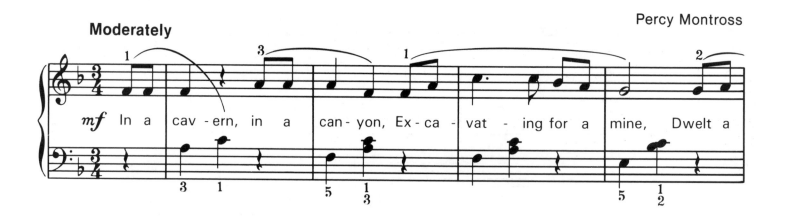

In a cav-ern, in a can-yon, Ex-ca-vat-ing for a mine, Dwelt a

min-er, for-ty- nin-er, And his daugh-ter, Clem-en-tine. Oh my

dar-lin', Oh my dar-lin', Oh my dar-lin' Clem-en-tine, You are

lost and gone for-ev-er, Dread-ful sor-ry, Clem-en-tine!

*The eighth notes may be played a bit unevenly, long short, long short.

Use after page 74.

WALTZ
Op. 39, No. 15

Johannes Brahms

GIVE MY REGARDS TO BROADWAY

Use after page 75.

Words and Music by
George M. Cohan

Give my re - gards to Broad - way, Re -

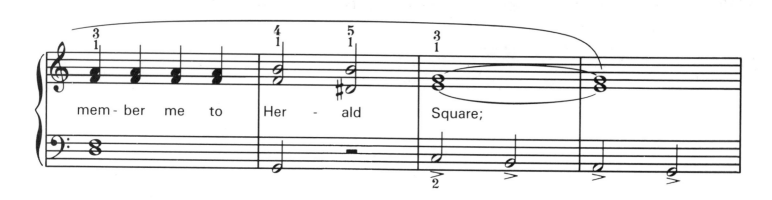

mem - ber me to Her - ald Square;

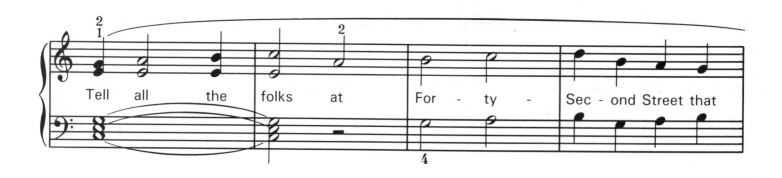

Tell all the folks at For - ty - Sec - ond Street that

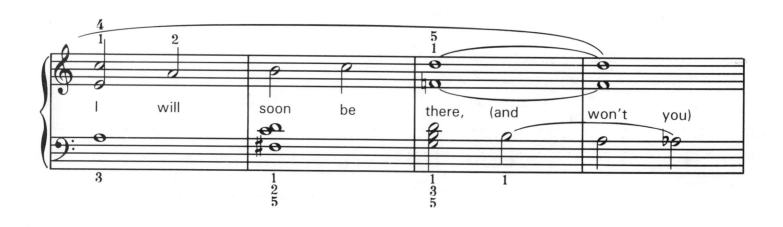

I will soon be there, (and won't you)

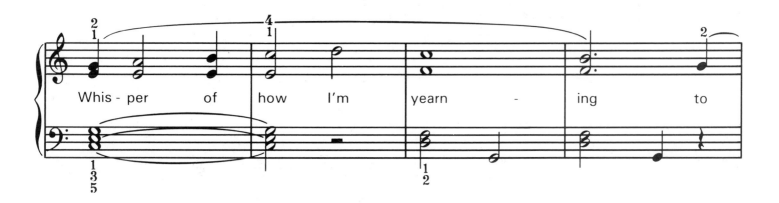

Whis - per   of   how   I'm   yearn - ing   to

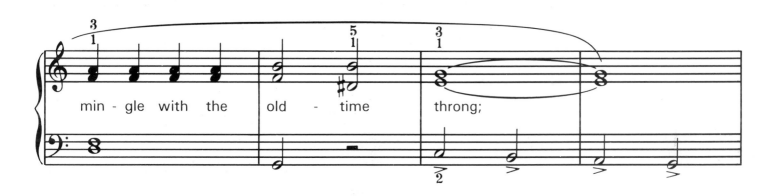

min - gle   with   the   old - time   throng;

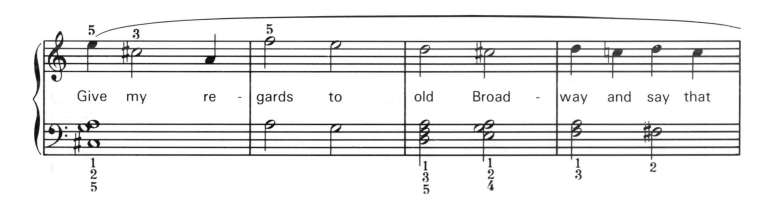

Give   my   re - gards   to   old   Broad - way   and   say   that

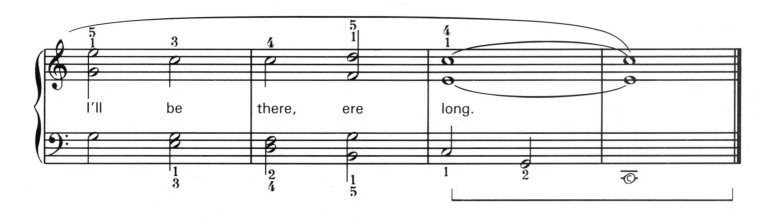

I'll   be   there,   ere   long.

CHINATOWN, MY CHINATOWN

Use after page 75.

Words by William Jerome
Music by Jean Schwartz

Moderately

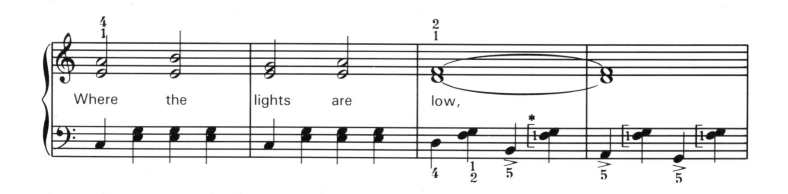

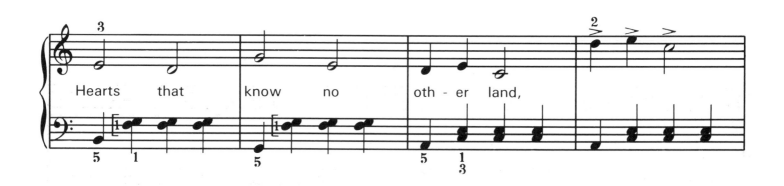

*Play the F & G with the side tip of the thumb.

WAITING FOR THE ROBERT E. LEE

Use after page 75.

Words by Wolfe Gilbert
Melody by Lewis F. Muir

Brightly

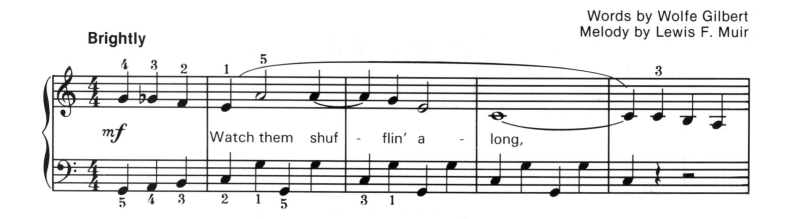

Watch them shuf - flin' a - long,

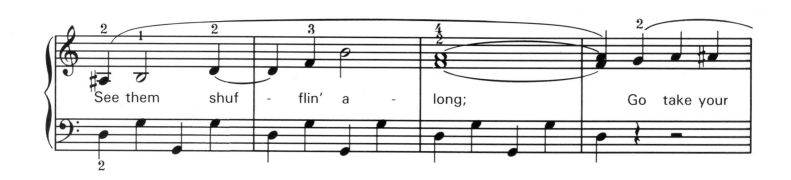

See them shuf - flin' a - long; Go take your

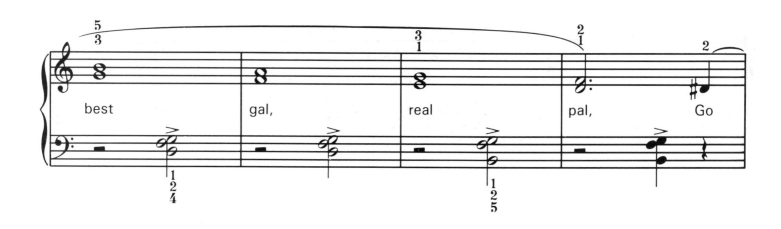

best gal, real pal, Go

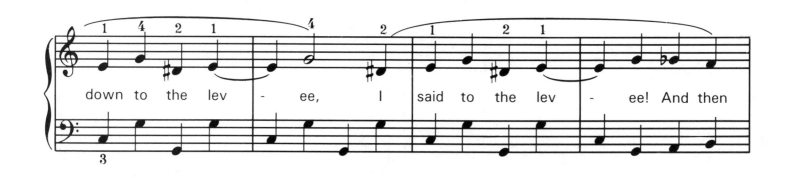

down to the lev - ee, I said to the lev - ee! And then

join that   shuf - fl - in'   throng,

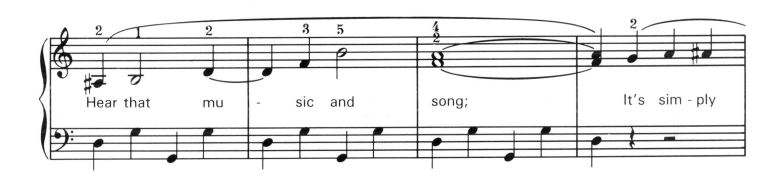

Hear that   mu - sic and   song;   It's sim - ply

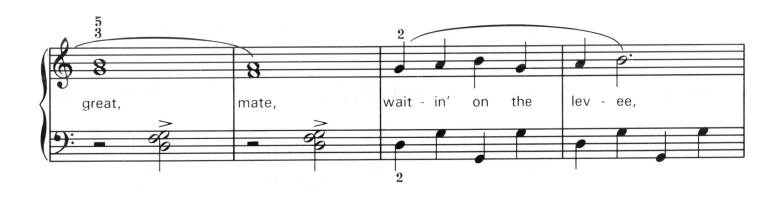

great,   mate,   wait - in'   on the   lev - ee,

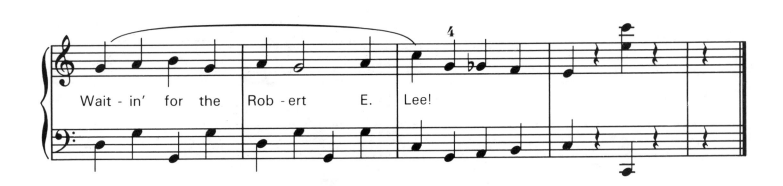

Wait - in' for the Rob - ert E. Lee!

I Am the Very Model

(from "Pirates of Penzance")

Use after page 75.

Gilbert and Sullivan

MARCHE MILITAIRE
(Theme)

Use after page 75.

Moderately fast march tempo

Franz Schubert

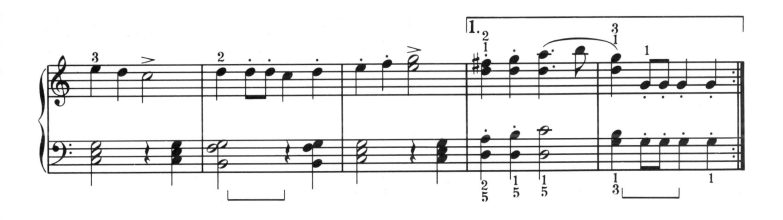

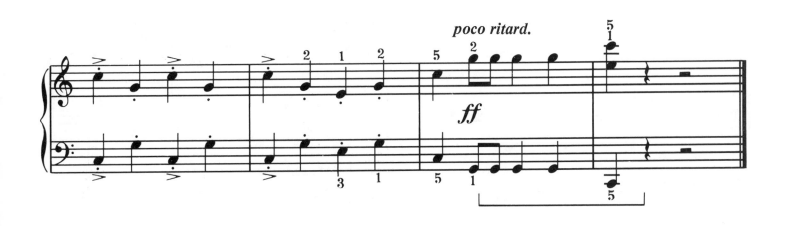

Happy Birthday to You!

Use after page 76.

Moderately

Mildred J. and Patty S. Hill

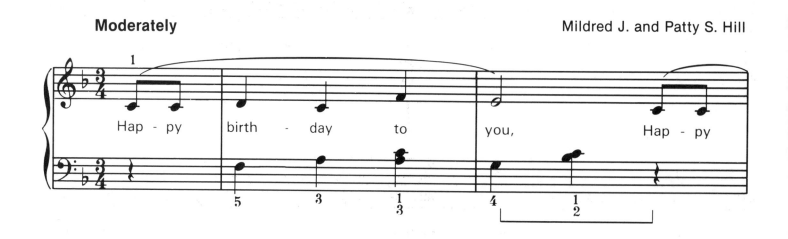

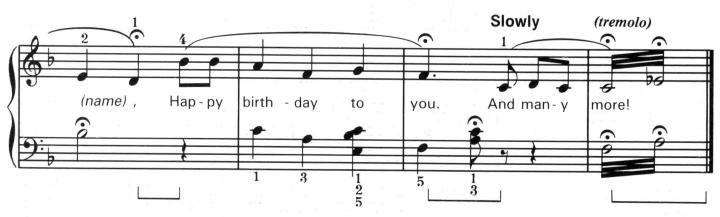

Use after page 76.

AULD LANG SYNE

Old Scottish Air
Words by Robert Burns

Moderately slow

FOR HE'S A JOLLY GOOD FELLOW

Use after page 76.

Traditional

D.S. 𝄋 al Fine

SHINE ON, HARVEST MOON

Nora Bayes
and Jack Norworth

Moderately slow

*The eighth notes should be played a bit unevenly, long   short, long   short.
**Play F & G with the side tip of the thumb.

ESPAÑA
(Themes)

Use after page 76.

A. E. Chabrier

Brightly

f

LH staccato

1. *(to next strain)* **2.**

mf

Fine

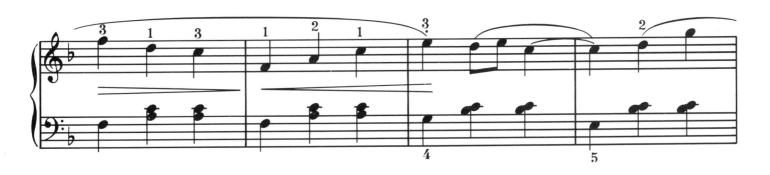

D.C. al Fine

ALEXANDER'S RAGTIME BAND

Use after page 76.

Irving Berlin

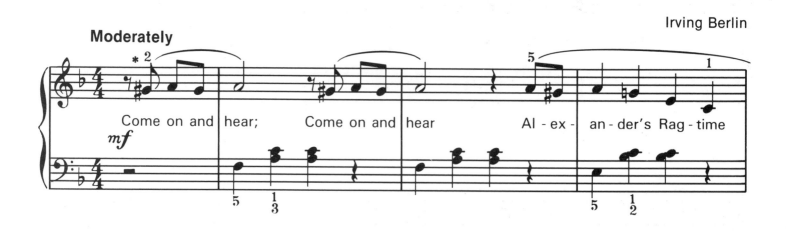

*The eighth notes may be played a bit unevenly, long   short, long   short.

OH! YOU BEAUTIFUL DOLL

Use after page 76.

Words by A. Seymour Brown
Music by Nat D. Ayer

Rhythmic

Oh! You beau-ti-ful doll, you great big beau-ti-ful doll!

Let me put my arms a-round you,

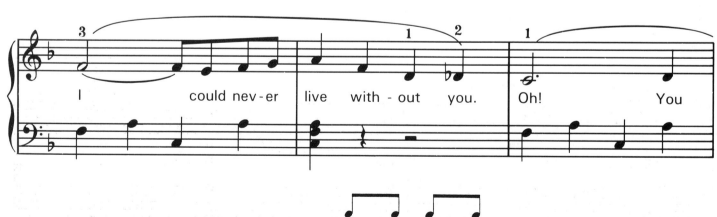

I could nev-er live with-out you. Oh! You

*The eighth notes may be played a bit unevenly, long short, long short.

**Play the F & G with the side tip of the thumb.

beau-ti-ful doll, you great big beau-ti-ful doll! If you

ev - er leave me, how my heart would ache, I want to hug you but I

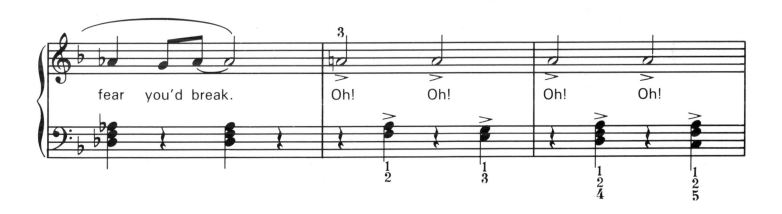

fear you'd break. Oh! Oh! Oh! Oh!

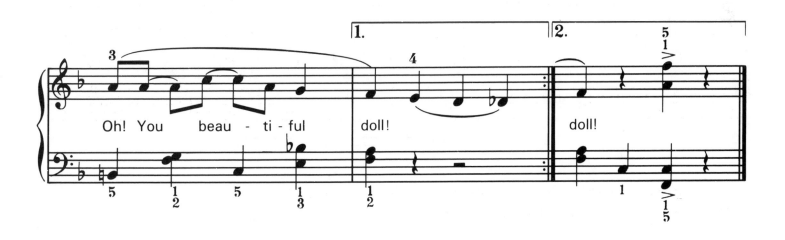

Oh! You beau - ti - ful doll! doll!

THANK GOD I'M A COUNTRY BOY

Use after page 76.

Words and Music by
John Martin Sommers

Moderately

*‖ = Make a slight pause after the *fermata* (𝄐).

CHORUS

Well, I got me a fine wife, I got me old fid-dle, When the

sun's com-in' up I got cakes on the grid-dle; And life ain't noth-in' but a

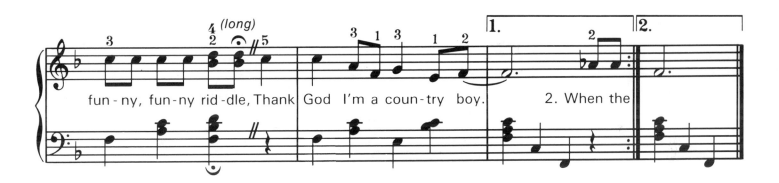

fun-ny, fun-ny rid-dle, Thank God I'm a coun-try boy.   2. When the

VERSES

2. When the work's all done and the sun's settin' low
   I pull out my fiddle and I resin up the bow.
   But the kids are asleep so I keep it kinda low:
   Thank God I'm a country boy.
   I'd play "Sally Goodin'" all day if I could,
   But the Lord and my wife wouldn't take it very good.
   So I fiddle when I can and I work when I should:
   Thank God I'm a country boy.
   (Chorus)

3. I wouldn't trade my life for diamonds or jewels,
   I never was one of them money hungry fools.
   I'd rather have my fiddle and my farmin' tools:
   Thank God I'm a country boy.
   Yeah, city folk drivin' in a black limousine,
   A lotta sad people thinkin' that's mighty keen.
   Well, folks, let me tell you now exactly what I mean:
   I thank God I'm a country boy.
   (Chorus)

4. Well, my fiddle was my daddy's till the day he died,
   And he took me by the hand and held me close to his side.
   He said, "Live a good life and play my fiddle with pride,
   And thank God you're a country boy."
   My daddy taught me young how to hunt and how to whittle,
   He taught me how to work and play a tune on the fiddle.
   He taught me how to love and how to give just a little:
   Thank God I'm a country boy.
   (Chorus)

Put Your Arms Around Me, Honey

Use after page 76.

Words by Junie McCree
Music by Albert von Tilzer

Moderately bright

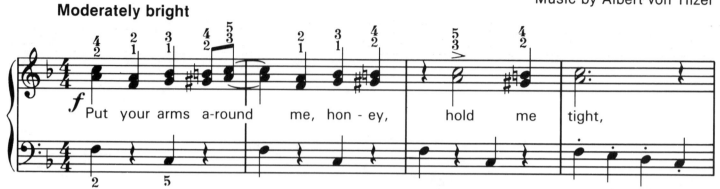

Put your arms a-round me, hon-ey, hold me tight,

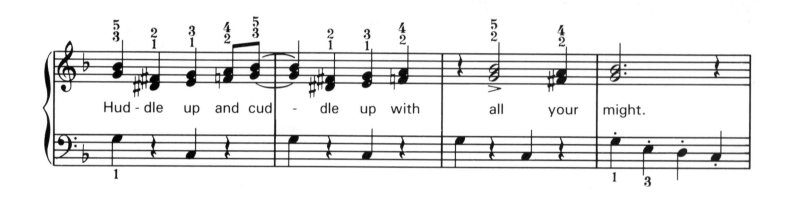

Hud-dle up and cud - dle up with all your might.

Oh! Oh! Won't you roll those eyes,

Eyes that I just i-dol - ize.

When you look at me   my heart be - gins to   float,

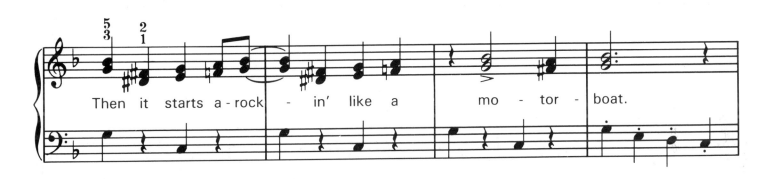

Then it starts a - rock - in' like a   mo - tor - boat.

Oh!   Oh!   I nev - er knew   an - y

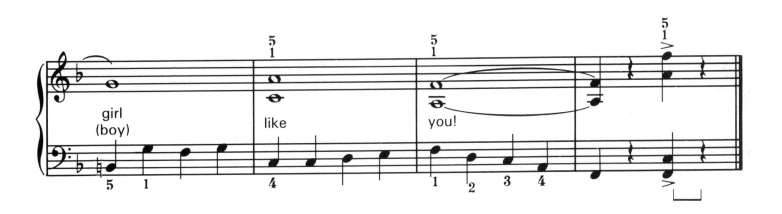

girl (boy)   like   you!

GUANTANAMERA

Use after page 78.

Moderately slow

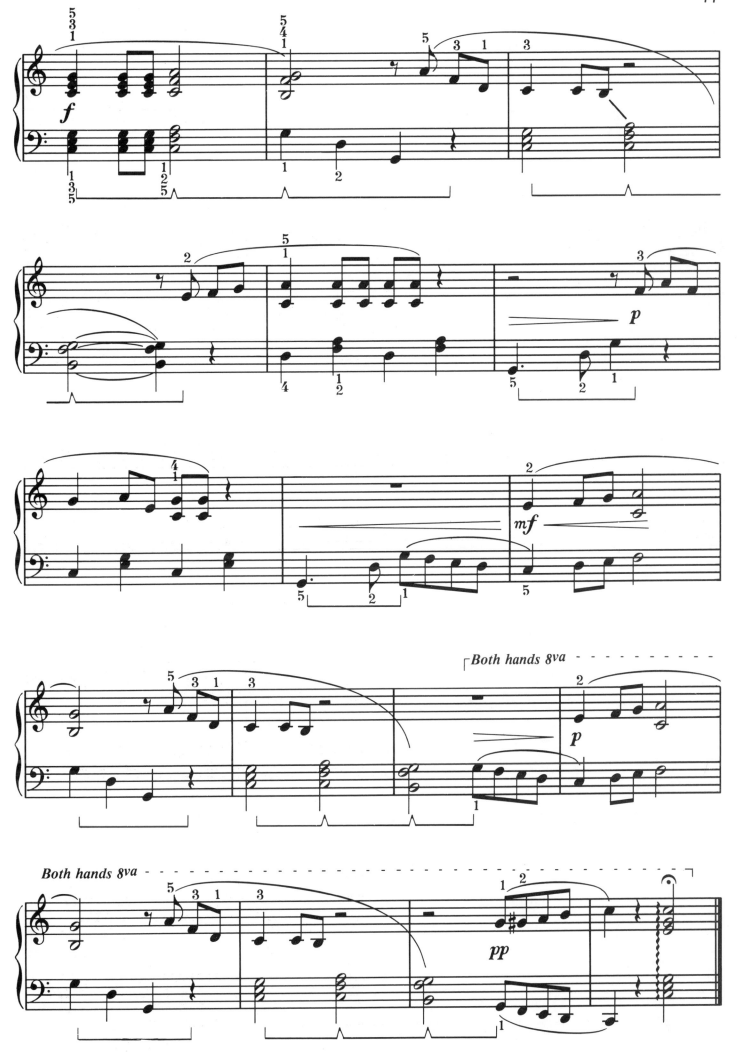

Come Back, Liza

Words and Music by
Irving Burgie and William Attaway

Moderate Calypso tempo (with much feeling)

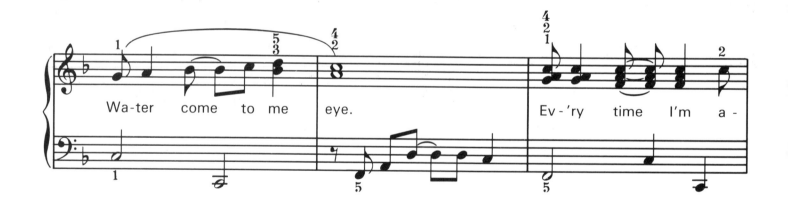

CHORUS

Come back, Li - za, come back, girl, Wipe the tear from me

eye, Come back, Li - za, come back, girl,

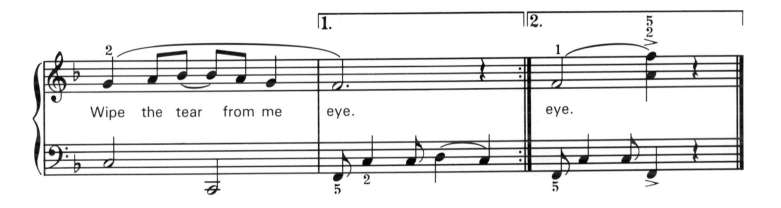

Wipe the tear from me eye. eye.

VERSES:

2. I remember when love was new, water come to me eye.
   There was one but now there's two, water come to me eye.
   (Chorus)

3. When the evening starts to fall, water come to me eye.
   I need to hear my Liza's call, water come to me eye.
   (Chorus)

4. Standing there in the market place, water come to me eye.
   Soon I'll feel her warm embrace, water come to me eye.
   (Chorus)

5. In the shadow I stand a while, water come to me eye.
   Soon I'll see my Liza smile, water come to me eye.
   (Chorus)

Use after page 82.

Annie's Song

Words and Music by
John Denver

2nd Verse:

Come let me love you, let me give my life to you,
Let me drown in your laughter, let me die in your arms.
Let me lay down beside you, let me always be with you.
Come let me love you, come love me again.

3rd Verse: Same as 1st verse.

Use after page 82.

SUNSHINE ON MY SHOULDERS

Words by John Denver
Music by John Denver, Mike Taylor and Dick Kniss

Ped. simile means "continue pedaling in the same manner."

2nd time D.S. 𝄋 al ⊕ Coda

give to you a day just like to - day.

If I had a song that I could sing for you, I'd

sing a song to make you feel this way.

⊕ CODA

Sun - shine al-most all the time makes me high.

Sun - shine al-most al - ways. . . .

2nd Verse: If I had a tale that I could tell you,
I'd tell a tale that's sure to make you smile.
If I had a wish that I could wish for you,
I'd make a wish for sunshine all the while.

D.S. 𝄋 al ⊕ Coda means repeat from the sign 𝄋 and play to the sign ⊕, then skip to the *CODA* (ending).

"WILLIAM TELL" OVERTURE
(Theme from the FINALE)

Use after page 84.

G. Rossini

Brightly

D.C. al ⊕, then CODA means repeat from the beginning, play to the sign ⊕, then skip to the *CODA* (ending).

PIANO CONCERTO IN A MINOR
(Theme from the 1st Movement)

Use after page 84.

Moderately fast

Edvard Grieg

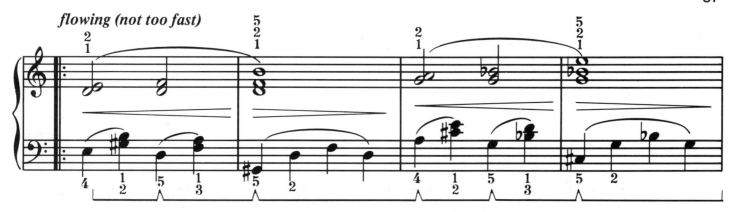

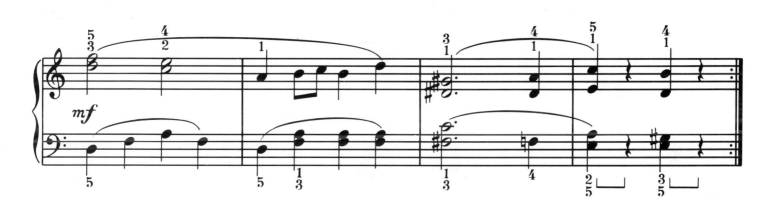

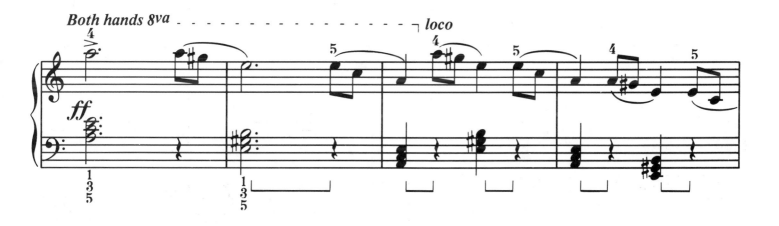

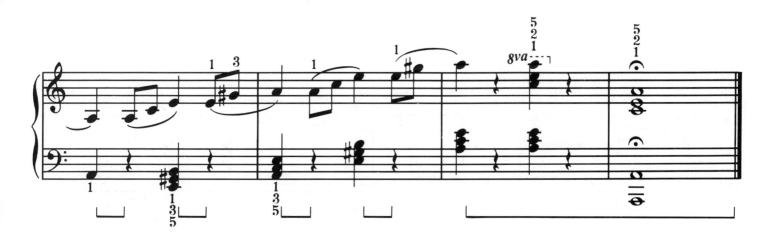

Use after page 88.

HUNGARIAN DANCE NO. 5

Johannes Brahms

Moderately fast

SOME OF THESE DAYS

Use after page 88.

Shelton Brooks

Moderately

Some of these days, you'll miss me, hon - ey.

Some of these days, you'll feel so lone - ly.

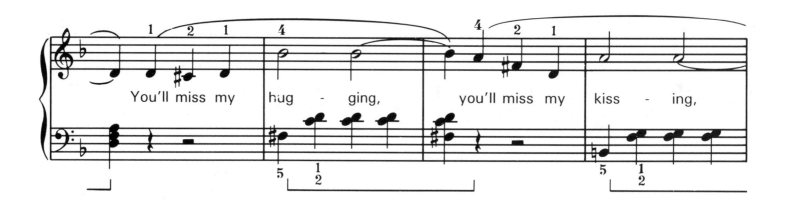

You'll miss my hug - ging, you'll miss my kiss - ing,

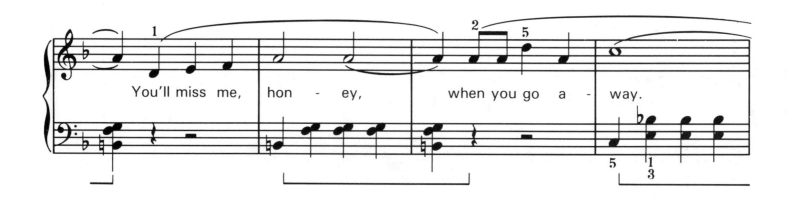

You'll miss me, hon - ey, when you go a - way.

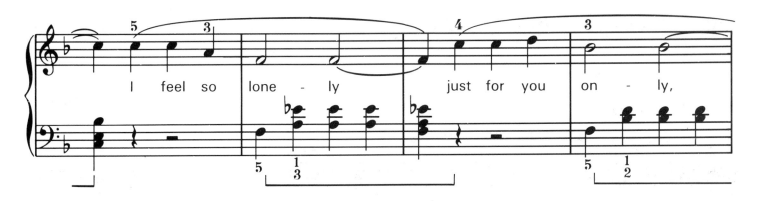

I feel so lone - ly just for you on - ly,

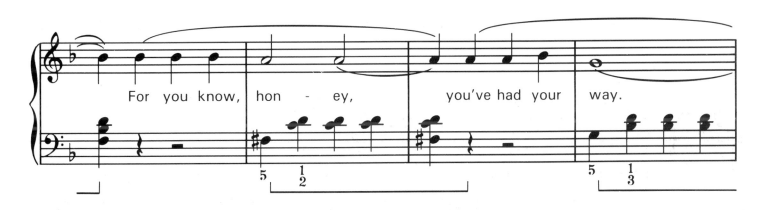

For you know, hon - ey, you've had your way.

And when you leave me I know 'twill grieve me,

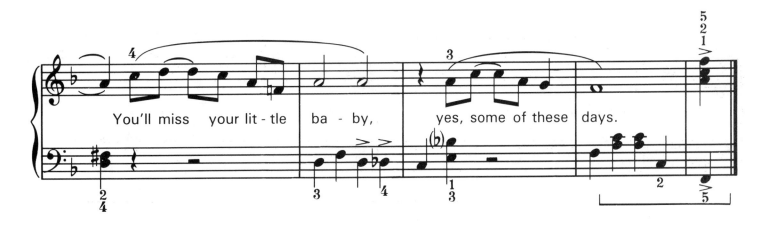

You'll miss your lit - tle ba - by, yes, some of these days.

Theme from
SOLACE
(A Mexican Serenade)

Use after page 92.

Very slow march time

Scott Joplin

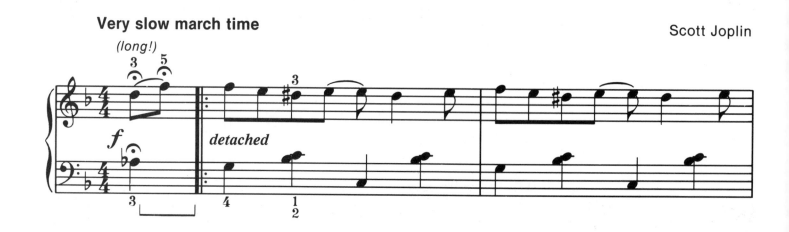

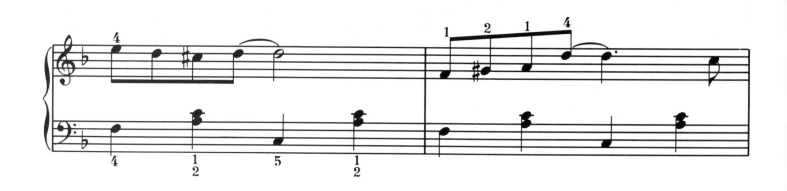

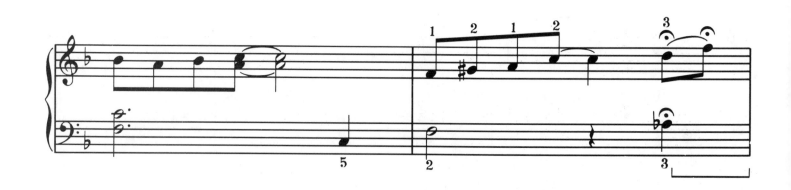

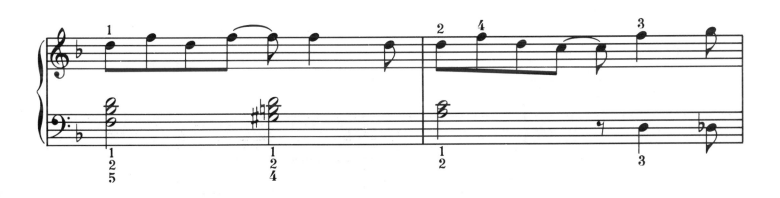

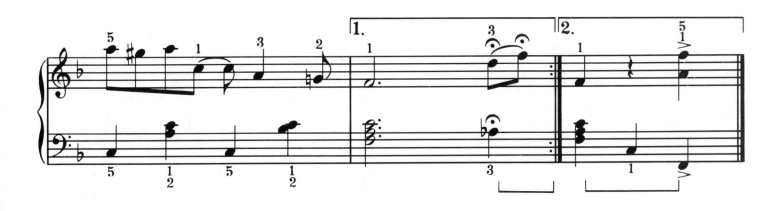

Day-O
(Banana Boat Song)

Use after page 94.

Words and Music by
Irving Burgie and William Attaway

Moderate Calypso tempo

Come, mis-ter tal-ley man, tal-ly me ba-na - na, Day-light come and me wan' go home.

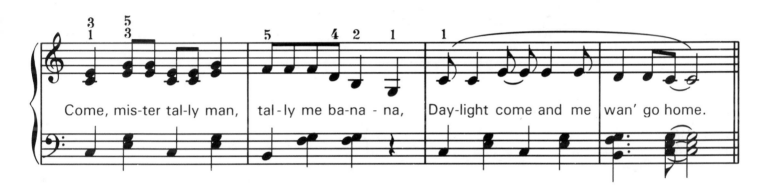

Come, mis-ter tal-ly man, tal-ly me ba-na - na, Day-light come and me wan' go home.

Freely

Day, me say day, me say day, me say day, me say day, me say day - o.

In tempo

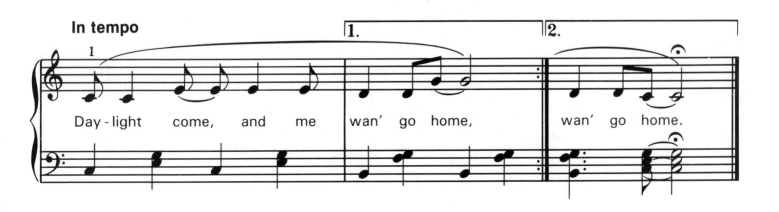

Day-light come, and me wan' go home, wan' go home.

"ANVIL CHORUS" THEME
from "Il Trovatore"

Use after page 94.

Giuseppi Verdi

Majestically